Galicia

Editorial Everest would like to thank you for purchasing this book. It has been created by an extensive and complete publishing team made up of photographers, illustrators and authors specialised in the field of tourism, together with our modern cartography department. Everest guarantees that the contents of this work were completely up to date at the time of going to press, and we would like to invite you to send us any information that helps us to improve our publications, so that we may always offer QUALITY TOURISM.

QUALITY
TOURISM
WITH
EVEREST

Please send your comments to:
Editorial Everest. Tourism department
Apartado 339 – 24080 León (Spain)
E-mail: turismo@everest.es

Editor: Raquel López Varela

Editorial coordination: Eva María Fernández, Irene Penas

Text: Rubén Camilo Lois González

Photographs: Miguel Sánchez and Puri Lozano, Imagen Mas, José Salgado and Archivo Everest

Cover design: Alfredo Anievas

Translated by: Babyl Traducciones

Maps: © Everest

© EDITORIAL EVEREST, S. A.
Carretera León-La Coruña, km 5 - LEÓN
ISBN: 84-241-0472-2
Legal deposit: LE. 108-2004
Printed in Spain

EDITORIAL EVERGRÁFICAS, S. L.
Carretera León-La Coruña, km 5
LEÓN (Spain)

www.everest.es
Atención al cliente: 902 123 400

Amongst the most attractive and original regions of Spain and indeed of the Iberian Peninsula is the **Autonomous Community of Galicia.** Dominated by the Atlantic and its rain but linked to a predominately Mediterranean landmass plagued by scarcity of water. A mountainous area with profoundly green landscapes that contrast with the flat plateaux and ubiquitous ochres of the neighbouring region of Castile. This north-western corner of Spain has historically had problems in communicating with the rest of the country (a continuous mountain barrier separates Lugo and Ourense from the Spanish Meseta and Asturias). Conversely, the way to Portugal is easy through the wide valley of the River Miño or over the highish ground that lies between Ourense and Tras-Os-Montes. In fact, a glance at any map makes it obvious that Galicia is an anomaly, the only territory on the Atlantic side of the Iberian peninsula not included within the state of Portugal.

In Spanish terms, both its dimensions (29,434 km^2) and its total population (2,742,622 inhabitants in 1996) make Galicia a medium-sized region. It is often said that Galicia is similar in size to Belgium and Denmark. However this comparison does not extend to its population: as a result of extensive outward migration and a traditionally low level of industrialisation, its current population is very much lower than either of these two European nations. However, its 92.8 inhab./km^2 of demographic density is still above the Spanish average, although this masks some marked contrasts between relatively highly populated coastal and riverine areas and a largely abandoned rural hinterland.

A mountainous green landscape, similar to that of Cervantes shown here, typifies the Community of Galicia.

The Galician population shows some marked contrasts of distribution between a sparsely populated hinterland and a highly populated coastal area. Above, Degrada. Below, Combarro.

Potato planting at Robledo de Rao. Agriculture and livestock breeding are still very important to the Galician economy.

Galicia's existence as a geographical unit goes back to Roman times, specifically to the 2nd century A.D. It was then a province of the Empire on a par with Lusitania, Baetica, Carthage and Tarraco. The *Gallaecia* of that era was much larger than today's region. It extended from the Duero over what is currently the north of Portugal to the centre of what is now Asturias, just short of the city of Leon. By the middle ages this had become the Kingdom of Galicia, first allied with the Asturian-Leonese monarchy and then with the Kingdom of Castile. Some key figures of the period, including Alfonso VII, Alfonso X "the Wise" and Afonso Henriques, founder of Portugal, took their first steps in the arts of government in Galicia, which was sometimes known to act independently of its neighbours.

To the right, landing fish at Portonovo. Fishing is the other great cornerstone of the Galician primary sector.

Padrenda, Hórreo (grain store).

With the arrival of the Catholic Monarchs and the introduction of a series of centralising measures, Galicia was effectively integrated first into the Crown of Castile and then in the 18th century into the Kingdom of Spain, then ruled by the first Bourbons. However, its isolation and chronically bad communications with the rest of the territory meant that Galician society continued to function as an inward-looking peasant society, where only the political and social elites were conscious of their place within a wider political unit.

Galician seafood enjoys a well-deserved reputation throughout Spain.

The mid-19th century saw the birth of a strong pro-independence movement in Galicia. Personalities like Rosalia de Castro, Manuel Murguía and Eduardo Pondal led an ideological and cultural movement known as the *Rexurdimento*. Castelao, Alexandre Bóveda, Otero Pedrayo and Vicente Risco gave further proof of the *galeguismo* that flourished in the 1920s and during the Second Republic. The movement reached its peak with the achievement of a Statute of Autonomy that was approved by a plebiscite in 1936. Immediately afterwards, the Spanish Civil War broke out and the process was suspended. However, in the Spanish Constitution of 1978 and the Statute of 1981, Galicia finally won self-government on the grounds of its historical nationality.

Portrait of Rosalia de Castro.

The Nobel prize-winner Camilo José Cela.

Statue of Emilia Pardo Bazán in the Méndez Núñez Gardens (A Coruña).

Galicia's individuality and peripheral situation have posed a series of practical difficulties for the introduction of Spanish as official language. Even today according to official statistics 65% of Galicians prefer to speak Galician, and more than 99% claim to understand and express themselves equally well in their own language and in Spanish. So it is little wonder that Galician literature is blessed with both a long history and an exceptionally productive present. This embraces such unexpected treasures as its remarkable collection of medieval poetry (including that of Alfonso X of Castile and King Dinís of Portugal), the poetic works of Rosalia de Castro in the second half of the 19th century, and the writings of R. Otero Pedrayo, V. Risco, E. Blanco Amor and A. Cunqueiro, among others, in the 20th century. Present-day authors like X. L. Méndez Ferrín, Manolo Rivas and Suso de Toro are all well known outside Galicia's borders.

Muscles, among the most highly-prized Galician produce.

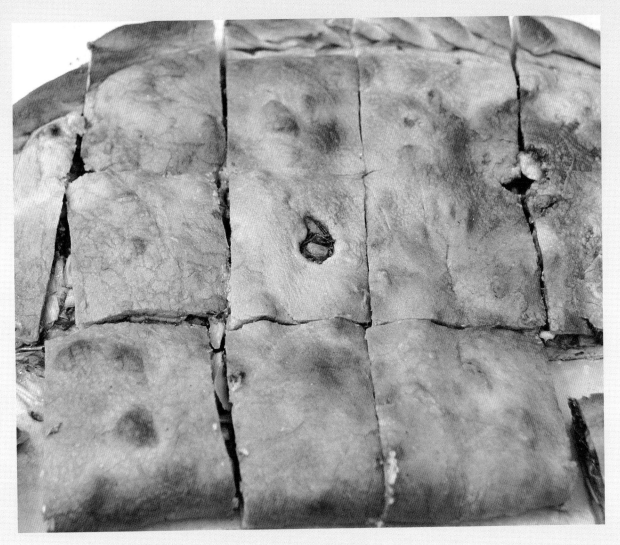

The empanada gallega can contain a great variety of fillings.

Exquisite Galician seafood.

Other Galicians have contributed to literature in the Spanish language: Nobel prize-winner Camilo José Cela and Gonzalo Torrent Ballester, to name but two. But Galician culture also takes another form: gastronomy, a field where the region has earned an enormous reputation. The overriding feature of Galician cuisine is its simplicity. In the face of such abundance and variety of seafood and fresh fish, the preferred methods are boiling or grilling, with at most the addition of a mild *sofrito* (lightly-fried onion base). The norm is to respect the flavour of fresh food. And its quality, like that of the local beef, consumed before the animal reaches 6-7 months of age. In wines, whites take pride of place, with the trio of Ribeiro, Albariño (D.O. Rías Baixas) and Valdeorras as the most important.

To the left, oysters au natural.

Among the best-known Galician wines are the denominations Ribeiro, Valdeorras, Rías Baixas and Ribeira Sacra.

Vineyards in Acuña.

A Coruña

The province of A Coruña is the most populous in Galicia and the only province with more than a million inhabitants. This makes sense if we bear in mind that it includes three important cities, A Coruña, Santiago de Compostela and Ferrol. We start our itinerary in the capital of the Autonomous Community, Santiago, whose artistic and cultural heritage makes it the authentic *jewel in the crown* of Galicia. Next we take a look around A Coruña and its attractive coasts, then Ferrol taking in the whole of the north of the province. Finally, we propose a short itinerary through the least built-up areas of the coast, from the Peninsula do Barbanza (between the rivers Arousa and Noia-Muros) to Fisterra (perhaps better known as Finisterre) and ending at the Costa da Morte (literally Coast of Death) in Malpica.

Cabo Fisterra
(Cape Finisterre).

Hórreo at Ozón in Muxía,
one of the biggest in Galicia.

View of Santiago de Compostela.

Santiago de Compostela was founded at the start of the Middle Ages as a shrine. Its purpose was to attract hundreds of thousands of pilgrims to its cathedral to venerate the remains of the Apostle Santiago (James), supposedly brought here from Palestine. The symbolic centre of the city is the Praza do Obradoiro square, which today boasts a kaleidoscope of architectural styles: Romanesque (the exterior of the Pazo de Xelmírez and the interior of the cathedral), Gothic (the front of the College of San Xerome, today the University rector's office), Renaissance (the Hostal dos Reis Católicos), Baroque (the façade of the cathedral) and Neo-Classical with heavy French influence (the Pazo de Raxoi, headquarters of the Presidency of the Xunta (regional government) and the Ayuntamiento (local government)). The square also houses the seats of the city's leaders: the president of the region, the mayor, the archbishop and the university rectorate.

The conveyance of the body of Santiago by sea from the Palestinian port of Jaffa to Iria Flavia in Galicia. Polychrome alabaster on an English 15th-century altarpiece. Santiago Cathedral Museum.

The cathedral was simultaneously the culmination of Romanesque style and the setting for the first serious attempt at transition towards the Gothic. Of note are its three naves, with triforia and galleries sometimes used in their day by pilgrims as dormitories. Also the decoration of the Portico de Praterías, with figures rarely found in Romanesque: King David, and another figure generally considered to represent the "woman taken in adultery" (with a skull, possibly an allegory of death).

*Santiago de Compostela.
Praza do Obradoiro.*

Santiago de Compostela. Façade of the Pazo de Raxoi, forming the west side of the Praza do Obradoiro.

Santiago de Compostela. Rúa do Vilar. Rain is a natural part of the countryside around Santiago. ▶

Santiago de Compostela.
Pórtico da Gloria.

To the right, Santiago de Compostela. View
of the cathedral from the north-eastern
corner of A Quintana: Puerta Santa and Torre
del Reloj.

Santiago de Compostela. The apostles Pedro (Peter),
Pablo (Paul), Santiago (James) and Juan (John), on the
right-hand pillar (facing the altar) of the central arch of
the Porch.

Gothic effectively began when the master
Mestre Mateo first introduced the smile and
the confiding exchange of glances, in his
portrayal of the prophets on the Pórtico da
Gloria, although the central theme of the
frontage, the pantocrator, still belongs to
Medieval iconography. The cathedral itself,
however, is still essentially Romanesque,
although its exterior was later covered with a
riot of Baroque ornamentation.

Next to the Praza do Obradoiro are the squares of A Quintana, Acibechería and Praterías, rounding off this immensely important historical centre of old Santiago. In A Quintana, a former cemetery, Galician Baroque reached its height, as it did both on the façade funded by the nuns of the closed order of San Paio de Antealtares, the exterior ornamentation of the cathedral, the Casa da Conga (built by the Cathedral Chapter) and the ornamentation on the upper part of the Casa da Parra.

Santiago de Compostela. Praza de Praterías.

*Plaza de A Quintana with
the Monastery of Antealtares.*

Santiago de Compostela. Plazuela de Fonseca.

*Santiago de Compostela. Façade of the
Hostal dos Reis Católicos.*

Santiago de Compostela. Casa de Parra.

Acibechería was the setting for a
dispute between the cathedral
and the monks of San Martiño
Pinario, administrators of the
highly profitable *voto de Santiago*
tax. The Archbishop forbad any
addition to the height of San
Martiño, a building already much
bigger than the cathedral itself.
Lastly, in Praterías, opposite the
cathedral, the Casa do Cabido
(chapter house) is a trompe d'oeil
structure, a luxuriously decorated
façade barely two and a half
metres thick.

*Santiago de Compostela. View
of the Praza de Acibechería
and the monastery of
San Martiño Pinario.*

Santiago de Compostela. Calle de San Francisco.

Santiago de Compostela.
Museo do Pobo Galego.

Santiago de Compostela.
Folk group outside the cathedral.

Santiago de Compostela.
Centro Galego de Arte Contemporánea.

Side by side with the historical and religious side of Santiago, the streets of Rúa do Vilar and Rua Nova are perfect expressions of the town's more commercial side. Their many colonnades offer shelter from the rain that falls on the city for an average of 164 days a year. Another attractive route for shoppers is that along Orfas-Caldeirería-O Preguntoiro near the old University building (today the Faculty of Geography and History), emerging into the Praza de Cervantes. In the northern area of the historic centre we recommend taking a look at the Renaissance palaces of Casas Reais and the adjoining market. Outside the city walls are the convents of San Francisco, San Domingos de Bonaval (with the Pantheon of Famous Galegos and beside it the Centro Galego de Arte Contemporánea arts centre) and of special note the Romanesque Collegiate Church of Sar.
A modern city has grown up beside this historic centre, as has an attractive South Campus of the University, reached by crossing the Alameda. Two short outings you can take from Santiago: to Padrón, at the mouth of the Ulla, where you can visit the House-Museum of Rosalia de Castro, set these days in the midst of some pepper plantations; and towards Ourense, in the *pazos* (country houses) of Oca and Ribadulla, the best examples of large Galician houses in rural settings, whose gardens are of great interest for their varied flora and formal layouts.

Santiago de Compostela. Auditorio de Galicia.

Santiago de Compostela.
Old collegiate church of Sar.

Santiago de Compostela. Praza de Cervantes, formerly
Praza do Campo. In the background, the Church of
San Benito.

Santiago de Compostela. Park of the Alameda.

A Coruña. Torre de Hércules and one of the "steel guardians" installed nearby.

To the right, A Coruña. Beaches of Riazor and Orzán.

A Coruña. Monument to María Pita, in the square of the same name.

A Coruña is remarkable for its almost totally seabound location. The city is set on a peninsula linked to the mainland by a narrow isthmus barely 200 metres wide that today forms the city centre.

Although its historical heritage cannot compare with that of Santiago, a stroll down its grand esplanade lets you admire the Atlantic in all its glory. This is a dangerous ocean, and in ancient times difficult to navigate. This is why the Torre de Hércules, a Roman lighthouse today covered with ornamentation from the time of Charles III, is the traditional emblem of the city.

A Coruña. Above, arcades in the Paseo de La Marina.

Below, Surfers' Fountain, on the beach at Orzán.

The region's capital city with more than a quarter of a million inhabitants experienced its greatest growth during the mid- to late-19th century. The Praza de María Pita dates from this era. The square once linked the upper part of the city with the district of A Pescadería, and the arcades of La Marina whose buildings, examples of popular Galician architecture, look out towards the sea as if obsessed with making the most of the few hours of sun. Modernism is also well represented in early-20th century La Coruña, the city of expansion, with Juana de Vega and the squares of Pontevedra, Lugo, Vigo and Juan Flórez. Perhaps the best examples to date from this period are the Kiosco Alfonso and, somewhat later, the La Terraza building, both set in the Méndez Núñez gardens. Any visit to this sector would not be complete without a tour of the fish and seafood stalls of the Plaza de Lugo and, if the heat begins to get to you, we recommend a swim from the city beach at Playa de Riazor.

A Coruña. Kiosco Alfonso.

A Coruña. Arcades in the Paseo de La Marina at dusk.

A Coruña. Playa de Riazor.

In the area around Riazor you will find the stadium of the same name, where the local team, Deportivo, holds its matches. There is also a magnificent example of a bourgeois garden city dating from almost a century ago. Outside A Coruña, the port of Sada deserves a visit and, in particular, its modernist *Terraza.* **Betanzos,** with its exceptionally well-preserved historic centre, still reminds us that it once competed with A Coruña for the status of principal city in the area. Further west, and wilder, the village of Caión and the beaches of Razo and Baldaio are also recommended, giving the visitor a foretaste of the Costa da Morte.

View of Betanzos.

Interior view of the Naval Museum at Ferrol.

Ferrol has long been unique in Galicia as much for its industrial initiative as for its relative isolation. In the 18th century the city's main powerhouse was its position as arsenal to the Navy. It later consolidated this military vocation by becoming an important centre of naval construction. As late as the early 1980s, more than 5,000 *Ferrolanos* were employed in its shipyard, a figure that has now fallen to the present 2,000. In recent years Ferrol has tried to diversify its industrial base, but problems of communication between the city and A Coruña and Santiago (currently being resolved) have effectively braked its economic development. On the way to Ferrol you can admire the magnificent landscapes of the Eume region and the River Ares. Also worth a visit is the historic centre of Pontedeume, at the heart of the Irmandiña revolt.

View of Cedeira.

The main attraction of Ferrol is its A Madalena district and the surrounding coastline. The district of A Madalena is one of the original districts of the town. It owes its completely regular shape and parallel and perpendicular streets to its designation as city centre during the 18ᵗʰ century. This followed the decision by the Spanish crown of the day to enhance the importance of this military settlement. What visitors find so striking in A Madalena is its stylistic richness and the variety of its arcades. On its coast, you really must visit the imposing Prior and Prioriño coves and its nearby beaches, exposed to the full force of the ocean.

To the north of Ferrol, you should make for the attractive port of **Cedeira,** with a beautiful beach with direct access from the town centre. And from there to the sanctuary of **San Andrés de Teixido,** because "those who do not go in life go after death". In this small town you can buy figurines made of bread and *herba de namorar* (love herb). Lastly, you should try to fit in **Estaca de Bares,** the most northerly point of the Peninsula, separating the Atlantic and the Cantabrian Sea.

On the **A Coruña shore,** and leaving aside the section from A Coruña to Bares, two main sections can be distinguished: the end of the Rías Baixas (the northern part of Arousa and Muros-Noia) and the Costa da Morte. The two are separated by Cabo Fisterra **(Cape Finisterre),** formerly considered the end of the known world, and where on a clear day we recommend you make a stop to watch the sunset.

Hermitage of San Andrés de Teixido.

Castro de Baroña.

A Pobra do Caramiñal.

*Palilleira making
the famous
Camariñas lace.*

Along right bank of the River Arousa is a string of fishing villages: **Rianxo, Boiro, A Pobra do Caramiñal** and above all **Ribeira,** whose sailors fish in seas all over the world. Between Ribeira and Noia try to stop off at the **Dolmen of Axeitos,** a megalithic funerary construction near Ribeira, and at the **Castro de Baroña,** a fort with a magnificent coastal location. **Noia** preserves evidence of its medieval past, including its Church of San Martiño and the town cemetery of Santa María A Nova. Nearby, **Muros** has preserved some very attractive historic streets and port installations that run back into the town itself, providing a convenient place for a stroll. North of Muros, the coast fronts the ocean itself. Here **Carnota**'s hórreo is worth a visit, and at near Fisterra you can make out the waterfall at the mouth of the River Xallas (only on Sundays, however, when the mini-power station that unfortunately uses its water is not working).

The **Costa da Morte** (Coast of death) is formed by a long stretch of the A Coruña shore, peppered with small fishing villages (Carariñas, Muxía, Laxe, Camelle, Corme, etc.). The whole area is very isolated and has a long history of shipwrecks, giving rise to its lugubrious name. This cliff-lined stretch is coast in its most savage state; the coast that must have been hugged by boats of old before striking out for the British Isles and France. Today we can take time out here to enjoy its wild countryside and learn about the many legends of accidents at sea, deliberately provoked or otherwise, associated with the area.

Hórreo at Carnota.

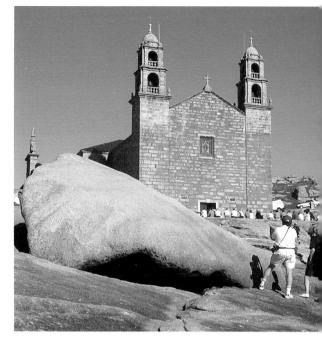

Sanctuary of Nosa Sañora da Barca (Muxía).

New Museum of Medieval "Laudas" in the Church of Santa María A Nova (Noia).

Muscle boats in the Ría de Arousa. ▶

Muscle gatherers at Muros

Pontevedra

Pontevedra takes in the part of the Galician coast with most tourism, the Rías Baixas; or at least, three of the four *rías* (river inlets) in the area (Pontevedra, Vigo and Arousa). The coast itself is fairly built up and includes the main centres of population. We therefore suggest that you first tour the city of Pontevedra and its *ría*, then Vigo and the southern part of the shore, and lastly the area around the River Arousa. We also give you an idea of the attractions of the inland provinces, although without establishing an exact itinerary. So whenever you need a break from your route along the coast at Pontevedra you can plan a trip inland.

In spite of being the capital of a dynamic and relatively rich province, **Pontevedra** is a city of modest proportions and the smallest of the seven principal Galician cities. This is due to the proximity of Vigo, where for two hundred years most of the urban growth in the Rías Baixas has been concentrated. Although in the 16th century the city was the most important fishing port in Galicia, in recent times it has lost its status as the chief landing place for the fleet, being replaced by the neighbouring town of Marín. Today, Pontevedra is a pleasant administrative and commercial centre whose industrial activities include the wood and chemical sectors. However, we must start by saying that after the exceptional case of Santiago de Compostela, Pontevedra boasts the most interesting historic city centre in Galicia.

Pontevedra. City Council building.

We can verify this by taking a stroll through its streets, stopping to admire its Baroque mansions, its traditional seafaring period houses and numerous emblazoned stately homes. The economic success of the city in more modern times is reflected in these buildings, now being restored.

Pontevedra. Praza da Leña. ▶

Pontevedra. Church of A Peregrina.

Pontevedra. Fountain in the Praza da Ferrería.

From a historical point of view the Praza da Ferrería and its 18th century Church of A Peregrina are of great interest. With its curious scallop shape, it maintains mainly Baroque features throughout its façade. The older Church of Santa María was funded by the powerful guild of *mareantes* (seamen), the owners of boats involved in catching sardines in what for the city was the prosperous 16th century. With a transitional style between Gothic and Renaissance, its façade takes the form of a stone altarpiece carved by the Dutchman Cornelis, with such notable scenes as *The dormition of the Virgin.*

In the historic centre is the Provincial Museum, one of the best-presented in Galicia. Here are exhibited proto-historic remains of the *Castrexa* period like the treasure of Caldas, a magnificent collection of painting and sculpture (Berruguete, Zurbarán, Murillo, etc.). Another curious feature of the Museum is an open-air exhibit in the form of the ruins of Santo Domingo, a magnificent example of local Gothic architecture.

The north bank of the Pontevedra River is the part of the region most popular with "sun and sand" tourists. The main centres are **Sanxenxo** and **Portonovo,** with a built-up Atlantic coastal area modelled on the Mediterranean style. Nearby, the area including the long open perspectives of the **A Lanzada beach** are also associated with ancestral fertility rites. Crossing the sandy reaches of A Lanzada we come to the coastal village of **O Grove** and the neighbouring island of **A Toxa.** Here was where some of the earliest experiments in spa tourism took place, in the 19th century, coinciding with the manufacture there of soaps and perfumes. Today A Toxa is well-tended spot, with its Grand Hotel, spa, casino, golf course and a series of tourist facilities that nevertheless manage to maintain an acceptable aesthetic quality.

Bueu.

A Lanzada beach.

Women mending nets at Bueu.

◀ *Island of Tambo, in the Pontevedra River.*

Island of San Simón, in the Vigo River.

In the middle of the Pontevedra river is the magnificent **Island of Tambo.** Southwards, on the left bank, lies the port of **Marín** with a series of beaches in its immediate area as well as the immaculate headquarters of the naval school. The next town, **Bueu,** is another typical fishing town, which has lost part of its charm due to recent building projects and which includes within its borders the Island of Ons, which is still inhabited and can be visited by boat in summer.

Vigo, with a population of almost 300,000 rising to nearly 500,000 if its immediate environs are included, is the biggest city in Galicia. The origin of its spectacular growth over the last two centuries is its port, better located than its rival Baiona within the river estuary, and which from the mid-18th century on established close communications with America. The port installations also encouraged its early industrialisation, based above all on the manufacture of conserves and naval construction. Later a complex industrial structure was to develop, with the arrival of car plants, ceramics and metallurgical factories, etc.

Starting our visit to the city at the port, one interesting stop is at the Marine Terminal from which we can admire the city's immense loading bays, and O Berbés, formerly the centre of Vigo's fishing industry but today in spite of its rather run-down in appearance an area full of fine restaurants. In the historical city centre - whose appearance has improved in recent years - is the Neo-classical co-cathedral and higher up, the Praza da Constitución.

Aerial view of the historic centre of Vigo.

Vigo. Pazo Quiñones de León.

Vigo. O Berbés.

Vigo, from Monte do Castro.

On interesting visit in this old district within the city walls is to the Mercado da Pedra market, with varied produce at good prices, and stalls of fresh oysters on Sunday mornings.

The city centre itself is defined by spacious streets and squares like the Porta do Sol, the Calle del Principe, Colón, the start of Gran Vía, García Barbón and Policarpo Sanz. This is the generous Vigo of the late-19th and early-20th centuries, extending towards the Alameda and with fine examples of Modernism like the García Barbón building. The whole of the district lies on the lower slopes of Monte do Castro, a proto-historical settlement and military fortress which long hindered the growth of the city centre.

Beyond O Castro extend the modern districts of As Travesas, Coia, A Florida, Castrelos and Fragoso, representatives of 1960s and 1970s Vigo. In Castrelos we find the oldest church in the city with its Gothic murals, and next to it the Quiñones de León Museum with interesting displays of archaeology and painting. Within the municipal boundaries you can enjoy peace and quiet and contact with nature on the Cíes Islands, with a permanent boat service to and from the city in summer.

The River Miño in the region of O Rosal (Pontevedra).

Aerial view of Baiona.

Aerial view of A Guarda.

Towards the south a visit to **Baiona** is a must. This historic town, popular with tourists, has an attractive and well-preserved centre and famous yachting club, and is also the setting for the Parador Condes de Gondomar hotel, housed in the splendid fortress of Monte Real. In Baiona the Rías Baixas come to an end. Following the coast towards Portugal, we reach the port of **A Guarda,** which specialises in shellfish, and the hill of **Santa Tegra** with a beautiful *Castrexo* settlement and magnificent views over the estuary of the Miño. Inland, the defensive and episcopal settlement of **Tui** also offers a good opportunity to enjoy historical buildings, ranging from a cathedral-fortress to several urban mansions and some fairly well-maintained monuments.

Fort of Santa Tegra.

View of Tui.

Stone cross on an island in the River Arousa.

The coast of Pontevedra along which runs the **River Arousa** starts at the island of A Toxa. To the north as far as the estuary of the River Ulla that marks the boundary with A Coruña extends a rich stretch of coast, intensively cultivated both by land and sea. Rich because beside the Albariño vineyards and the fruit and vegetable farms the river is laid out in shallow beds in the form of platforms devoted to the breeding of muscles to the tune of some 45 metric tons per year. The muscles are submerged to allow them to feed, and secured to the platforms by a rope. We should bear in mind that Galicia produces 60% of the muscles in Europe, and that the greater part of the region's production is concentrated at Arousa.

Cambados.

A popular local legend tells that when the devil tried to tempt Jesus in the desert, he said: "I will give you everything except Fefiñáns, Cambados and San Tomé". These three towns, practically one, offer the best historical monuments in Arousa, with large mansions like that at Fefiñáns and a great number of emblazoned houses. In early August Cambados celebrates the festival of Albariño wine, and there are lots of opportunities to taste the fresh fish and seafood from the river. Near Cambados is the island of Arousa, today linked to the mainland by a modern bridge and still preserving many unique features. Vilagarcía de Arousa is the main centre of population and economic dynamism. Its port is one of the biggest in Galicia and it has permitted considerable industrial development in its immediate area. Although Vilagarcía is a modern town, it is still possible to find in its streets some wonderful examples of urban mansions and singular buildings in a style reflecting the transition between the 19th and 20th centuries. Some kilometres further north, the Torres do Oeste towers at Catoira remind us of how between the 8th and 12th centuries Galicia had to defend its coast from Norman and Viking invasions.

District of Deza.

Among the inland regions of Pontevedra, three are of particular interest: **Terra de Montes, Deza** and **Tabeirós.** The three form perfect examples of the transition towards the Galician hinterland without leaving the coastal area of the region. A Terra de Montes is reached by the Pontevedra-Ourense road, and a few kilometres out of Pontevedra we recommend a visit to the famous *carballeira* of San Xusto, often referred to in popular folklore. Then at Cerdedo and Forcarei, we enter the area of flower-growers, mule-keepers and *capadores* (hunters). These mountainous areas oblige many of their people to make their living at least part of year in activities other than agriculture. For those interested in history we must not forget the concentration of *hórreos* (grain stores) at Cerdedo, and the Monastery of Aciveiro in the district of Forcarei.

Muscle boats at Carril, in the Ría de Arousa.

Rapa das bestas at Sabucedo (A Estrada).

Romeria de O Corpiño, in Lalín.

Tabeirós is the name given to the region whose centre is **A Estrada,** a modern-looking and bustling place famous for its furniture industry and a gastronomic festival celebrating the salmon. South of the town of A Estrada in the parish of Sabucedo one of the best-known *rapas das bestas* in Galicia takes place every summer. The *rapa* is the cutting of the manes of the wild horses that live in the surrounding hills. The struggle between the young men of the parish and the animals, and the festival held around it, is one of the best live entertainments on offer in the territory of Pontevedra. Lastly, in the region of Deza, specifically in **Lalín,** you can go shopping for fashionable clothes at good prices in the outlets of Galician fashion designers (Florentino, Montoto, and many more). This inland area is well known for its skill at livestock breeding and for the cuisine on offer in its restaurants. Also for the processions of O Corpiño, which take place on the 23rd of June every year, and which supposedly cures souls possessed by the devil.

Lugo. Night view of the cathedral.

Lugo

In the provincial division of Spain promoted by Javier de Burgos, the new administrative units had to possess diverse geographical elements (coast, mountain, extensive river valleys, etc.). Lugo complies to perfection with this principle, extending as it does from north to south between the Cantabrian Sea and the valley of the Sil, with mountains to the east and a generous plain known by the expressive name of A Terra Chá (Flat Earth). Any overview of this territory must start with its ancient capital, and after that we suggest a trip to the north coast, another along the path of the pilgrim's way of the Camino de Santiago through the province, and a last trip to admire the River Sil and its steep banks.

*Virxe dos Ollos
Grandes, in Lugo
cathedral.*

The 1st century A.D. city wall of **Lugo** has recently been declared Heritage of Mankind. And rightly so, since this is a monument almost two thousand years old that remains practically intact, surrounding the historic centre of the city. Lugo is the oldest city in Galicia, with numerous Roman remains in its subsoil and nowadays in the well-stocked exhibits rooms of its Provincial Museum. We recommend starting your tour of the city with a turn round the city wall followed by a look round the museum.

The cathedral, started in Romanesque style and concluded with an original Neo-Classical façade, is also well worth a visit. This is a medieval building with three naves and triforium, and an ogival heading that reflects its Gothic origins. Of interest inside is the Baroque choir, with more than sixty seats in walnut wood with intricate ornamentation. The most venerated image here is the enormously expressive 15th century and in polychrome granite *Virxe dos Ollos Grandes,* (virgin with big eyes).

Praza Maior de Lugo.

Adjacent to the cathedral are some of the best sites in secular Lugo: the Episcopal Palace, the Baroque Praza do Campo square and the central Praza Maior, with its consistory house set in a Baroque mansion. Between the historical centre and the new districts of the town are the gates in the city wall, including the medieval gate of San Pedro, Porta Falsa and the Gates of Boquete and Miñá, with posterior modifications. On a much grander scale are the gates of Bispo Aguirre and Porta Nova, constructed little more than a century ago.

Y para comer... Lugo, (and for eating, Lugo), in the words of a sixties tourist slogan. This sentence summarises one of the undoubted main attributes of the city: the chance to enjoy magnificent meat and fish from A Coruña or the neighbouring Cantabrian coast at interesting prices. In Lugo, enormous quantities of octopus are consumed, above all at the beginning of October during the festivals of San Froilán, when most of the province's inhabitants and thousands more from nearby areas take part in what is generally considered to be the largest procession in Galicia. Before eating, any good Lugan will enjoy an aperitif of wine with tapas in any of the many bars lining streets like Calle da Cross, Nova, Miño and Bispo Basulto in the historic centre, or Recatelo and A Milagrosa somewhat further out. Even in winter you must sample the zorza (a very spicy pork mixture).

Interior of Santa Eulalia de Bóveda.

From the capital you should also fit in two
other brief visits. The first is to Santa Eulalia de
Bóveda, in a rural parish within the municipal
area, with an enigmatic Late Roman building
that has been variously described as a place of
entertainment, a space consecrated to an
eastern deity or a Paleo-Christian temple. The
second visit is one to the magnificent military
settlement of Viladonga, dating from the
Roman era. The Fort, on the road to Oviedo,
maintains its impressive structure intact and
has an interesting adjoining museum.

Lugo. Façade of the Casa Consistorial.

◀ *City wall of Lugo, declared Heritage of
Mankind by Unesco in 2001.*

Mondoñedo. Fiesta of Los Remedios.

View of Ribadeo. ▶

Praza do Campo (Ribadeo).

Playa de Foz.

A journey to the **coast** at Lugo will take you all day, even if you take the new road to Mondoñedo that lets you keep up a decent speed throughout A Terra Chá. **Mondoñedo** is a former bishop's seat and a historical city. Its general layout, its cathedral with its square are of particular interest. The cathedral combines the two most representative architectural styles in Galicia: Romanesque (the central body of the façade has the large rose window and cross-ribbed vaults of Gothic transition) and the Baroque (the twin towers that flank the façade and the high altarpiece). Mondoñedo is also a land of writers, Álvaro Cunqueiro among them, and of bakers, the proof of which is not in the pudding but in a special Mondoñedo cake. Towards the north-east we find **Vilanova de Lourenzá,** the site of an impressive monastery, and Ribadeo on the attractive River Eo that marks the boundary with Asturias. If you stop here you must not miss visiting the Praza do Campo, with the old Pazo de Marqués de Sargadelos mansion, today the Town Hall, the Church of Santa María, and the Casa de los Moreno, a magnificent example of early 20th century architecture.

Viveiro. Galleries.

From Ribadeo westwards, following the line of the coast, you cross a good stretch of beaches at **Rinlo, Barreiros** and **Foz,** the summer haunts par excellence of the Lugo coast. The shore then turns to cliffs, becomes industrialised or has been recently built-up. This has happened at **Burela,** a small whaling port until the 1970s, at present the largest settlement in the area and next to Bermeo is the largest tuna fishing centre on the Cantabrian Sea. Some kilometres further on are the remains of the old industrial areas only recently refurbished, at **Sargadelos,** and the new industrial activity of alumina-aluminium, a plant more than one kilometre long that processes bauxite brought in from Africa. **Viveiro** is a beautiful historical district and a prosperous commercial centre where traces of the old city wall can still be seen. Of note for their historical interest are the Renaissance Puerta de Carlos V and some Baroque mansions. The situation of Viveiro at the mouth of the Landro is magnificent, and you can admire it from the lookout point at San Roque.

Puerto del Poio. Monument to the Pilgrim.

O Cebreiro. Palloza.

Monastery of Samos.

The Camino de Santiago enters Galicia over the hills of O Cebreiro and, to be precise, the village of the same name is an excellent place for your first stop. **O Cebreiro** is a traditional rural settlement combining farmhouses with the older *pallozas,* dwellings that go back to proto-historic times. This town is associated with the legend of the Holy Grail, the transubstantiation of the body and blood of Christ during the consecration, in a 12th century chalice that is still preserved today. Towards Triacastela you cross one of the most difficult sectors of the Galician part of the Santiago trail. A few kilometres further on you reach the historical town of **Samos,** with its Pre-Romanic chapel of Del Ciprés and its Benedictine monastery with Baroque groundplan.

◀ *Ribadeo. Praia das Catedrais.*

Monastery of Samos. Cloister. ▶

Church of Portomarín.

Sarria is undoubtedly, the main Jacobean town in the province of Lugo. Among its most interesting buildings are the Church of San Salvador and the Convent of the Mercedarias or the Magdalena, its main monuments. You will also enjoy a visit to Portomarín, an emblematic village on the Path that was flooded by a dam several decades ago. Today it would have the appearance of any modern, typical mid-20th century village if it were not for the fact that its imposing Church of San Xoán, whose crenelated building expresses the power of the order of the Knights of Santiago, was transferred here to avoid the flooding. In the area of **Palas de Rei,** another church, Vilar de Donas, is a perfect example of the aesthetic qualities of rural Romanesque, its interior enriched by the presence of Gothic murals and late medieval tombs. Also in Palas is the Castle of Pambre, one of the few intact examples of a medieval fortress extant in Galicia.

Convent of the Magdelena (Sarria).

Castle of the Counts of Lemos,
at Monforte de Lemos.

The **Valley of the Sil** at Lugo, like the Orense side of the river, is known as *Ribeira Sacra*. *Ribeira* because the course of the Sil is channelled throughout this sector, running down over a steep terraced course to assist in the cultivation of the *Sacra* wine. Here you will find numerous examples of churches and monasteries of medieval origin, at places like Ferreira de Pantón, San Vicenzo, Pombeiro and San Estebo de Ribas de Miño. In summer, to enjoy this natural and historical environment, we recommend a trip in a catamaran, either down the River Sil or from Miño to Portomarín. **Monforte de Lemos** is the main town in the south of Lugo. A traditional railway centre, it has several historic buildings of considerable interest. On a mound that dominates the town is the Castle of the Counts of Lemos, and beside it the monastery of San Vicenzo do Pino. Of even greater interest is the Colegio de la Compañía, in Herrerian style, where two paintings by El Greco can be found. From Monforte eastwards you set off over the mountainous lands of O Courel, recreated by the poet Uxío Novoneyra, with their impressive natural landscapes, interesting tree-lined spaces (Devesa da Rogueira) and the first signs of slate mining in the area.

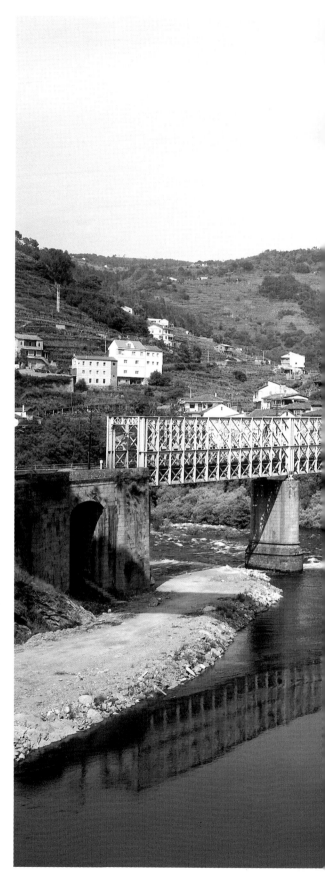

Estuary of the Sil at Miño, in the Ribeira Sacra.

Façades with colonnades in the historic centre of Ourense.

Ourense

The fact that the province of Ourense is the least affected by tourism in Galicia by no means indicates any lack of attraction. It only has two negative factors: this is the only inland administrative area, and it is not crossed by the part of the Path of Santiago from France. However, this "unknown" province has an impressive historical and natural heritage. We can briefly cite some of its landmarks by focussing first on the capital, then following an itinerary through O Ribeiro and A Arnoia, then through the mountainous parts of the province and, finally, through Valdeorras, or rather extreme eastern end of the territory at Valdeorras-O Bolo.

Ourense. As Burgas.

Ourense. Ponte Maior.

Ourense is the principal inland city in Galicia, with something more than 100,000 inhabitants. The city is built at a crossroads, on the only route from Sil in the north to A Limia, the Valley of Monterrei and the area of Chaves in the south; and from the mountains of Manzaneda and Queixa to Ribeiro and the foothills of the Dorsal. The city lies in the valley of the Miño, on a depression at the confluence of this river with its tributary the Barbaña. Ourense has existed since the times of the Romans, whose main interest lay in the spa waters at As Burgas. Waters that reach the surface at a high temperature and that even today we can enjoy in the historical city centre. The city assumed its present form during the early centuries of the Middle Ages, when its growth was enhanced by a bishopric interested in exploiting the rich land around it, in particular to grow vines.

Ourense. As Burgas (detail of spring).

Ourense. Cathedral.

Detail of one of the small statues carved in wood on the high altarpiece (Ourense cathedral).

A quick look round the Praza Maior reveals a magnificent collection of civil buildings of relatively recent origin (mostly 18th and 19th century) surprising for their harmony, and the typical colonnades and galleries of buildings in north-west Spain. After climbing through a honeycomb of narrow streets you reach the cathedral. This is an excellent example of Romanesque design, with three naves, although many decorative elements and parts of the building itself are Gothic, Renaissance (the grille that closes the main chapel and its very valuable altarpiece) and Baroque. In any case, the points of most interest in the cathedral are its 13th century Gothic transitional Pórtico del Paraíso, clearly influenced by the Pórtico da Gloria in Santiago. Perhaps the only negative element in this central building in historic Ourense is that none of its façades gives onto a large enough square or open space to let it be seen in all its splendour. The cathedral forms an integral part of the urban fibre of the historical centre, as was normal for large medieval religious constructions.

Near the cathedral is the monastery of San Francisco, with its outstanding Gothic cloister, also Santo Domingo, a 17th century work, and among the civil constructions the 16th century palace of Oca Valladares, today headquarters of one of the most emblematic socio-cultural institutions in the city, the Liceo Recreo. The historic centre is a great place for tasting sampling the wines of the Ribeiro, Monterrei and Valdeorras (three denominations of origin of the province) in its typical streets full of bars and pubs. Adjoining the centre, the park of San Lázaro is more like a typical inner-city square than the historic setting for the regular markets that take place on the outskirts of old Ourense.

One hundred years ago, the great thoroughfare of the city was Avenido Progreso, which is still a main road today. This street starts at the medieval bridge over the Miño from which we can view the sweep of this great Galician river as it runs through the town. Near Ourense we suggest two short outings: one to the exceptional Baroque **Monastery of Oseira,** of colossal dimensions and right next to the Path of Santiago; another, to the now heavily-restored **Allariz,** a medieval and Baroque town near A Arnoia.

Fiesta do Boi (Allariz).

Allariz. Panoramic view and bridge at Vilanova over the River Arnoia.

O Ribeiro and **A Arnoia** are two natural regions of Orense set in the valleys of twin rivers, the Miño and its tributary the Arnoia. The banks of the Miño form the most characteristic area of vineyards and wine production in Galicia.

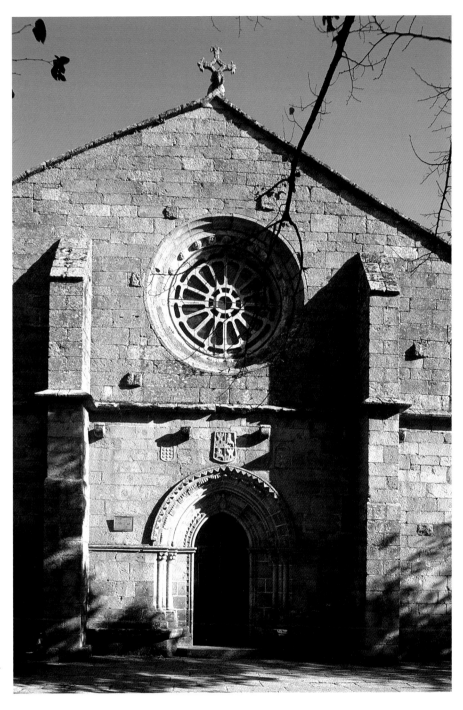

*Ribadavia. Church of
Santo Domingo.*

In spite of its historic city centre and medieval origins, Ribadavia is today an administrative centre. Proof of its vanished splendour are the remains of the 15th century castle of the Sarmiento family, and the former walled site known as the Jewish Quarter due to the importance of the Jewish community in the town. Of enormous importance in Ribadavia are its Festival of Wine and Festival of History. To the north, the **monastery of San Clodio,** near Leiro, preserves a magnificent 13th century Cistercian church. **O Carballiño,** modern in appearance, is well known for its large number of spas, the festival of the octopus that takes place in early August and the original Church of the Vera Cruz, work of Antonio Palacios.

Monastery of San Paio de Clodio, near Leiro.

Of interest in the adjoining region of A Arnoia are **Celanova,** with its large monastery of San Rosendo at its centre. This work expresses the magnificence achieved by the Galician Baroque. It also shows what can be done with a vast historical building in hosting public amenities in the present day (institutions, local government headquarters, employment offices, local associations, etc.). Inside San Rosendo, the small 10th century chapel of San Miguel is a jewel of Mozarab architecture. In Celanova we recommend a visit to the historical town of **Vilanova dos Infantes** and, a little further away, to the **Fort of Castromao,** inhabited between the 6th and 2nd centuries B.C. South of Celanova, towards Portugal, are the Church of Santa Comba de **Bande,** simple in form as befits a Visigothic building.

Roman Camp of Aquis
Quercuennis (Bande).

Monastery of Celanova.
Exterior of the Chapel
of Saint Miguel.

Most the **mountains of Ourense** are in this half of the province. Among these are the Manzaneda range, the mountains of Queixa, O Eixo, Segundeira and Pena Trevinca. This is a mountainous area whose summits rise to between 1,600 and 2,100 metres above sea level, and show obvious signs of quaternary glacial modelling. Certainly the best-known area of all is **Cabeza de Manzaneda,** with its comfortable installations site of the only skiing station in Galicia.

Chandrexa de Queixa, in the high lands of Ourense.

◀ *Ribadavia. Castle.*

Conversely, the high lands at Trevinca are not of much interest to visitors seeking contact with nature since the foothills of this mountain range where of most of the slate quarrying operations in Ourense take place. The more extensive Serra do Xurés reach the border with Portugal at Limia Baixa, the southernmost part of the province, marking the Spanish boundary of the **Parque Natural do Xurés** that continues as the Portuguese national park of A Peneda-Geres, a unique case of a protected space that spans two countries.

Winter station at Cabeza de Manzaneda.

Mountain landscape at Cabeza de Manzaneda.

Castro Caldelas. Castle.

Carnival of Laza, one of the oldest in Europe.

Detail of one of the "peliqueiros" in the
Carnival at Laza.

At the foot of the mountains are some small
settlements like **A Pobra de Trives, Castro
Caldelas** and **Manzaneda.** Of note in A Pobre de
Trives are examples of Hidalgo architecture: the
17th century Casa Grande and the 19th century
Pazo dos Marqueses. Castro Caldelas is
important for its recently restored castle, and
Manzaneda for the remains of its city wall,
which are still extant. In the southern foothills of
Queixa, the village of Laza on the road to Verín
and Xinzo de Limia, is the authentic capital of
Galician carnival *(entroido).*

O Barco de Valdeorras. General overview.

Valdeorras is a valley formed by the river Sil as it enters Galicia, and **O Bolo** is a mountainous area to its south. The two together make up the extreme east of Ourense, bordering on the neighbouring regions of Bierzo and A Cabrera. Valdeorras has a rich quarrying tradition, for these towns have the biggest reserves of slate in the entire world. Its wine production is also associated with a prestigious denomination. Over the years, the small town of **O Barco** has been bringing together the region's population in a modern centre, although it still preserves as part of its urban heritage the 17th century Pazo do Castro and the interesting monastery of Xagoaza. **A Rúa** is a long, winding town, headquarters of the main wine-growing cooperatives of Valdeorras although the best wine-growing landscapes are to be found on the terraced and steep lands, the *codos* of Larouco.

Towards O Bolo is the impressive sanctuary of As Ermidas, which is impressive both for the quality of its Baroque architecture and for its spectacular situation. Nearby, A Veiga and O Bolo appear dominated by twin fortresses and offer several interesting routes for pathwalking. Lastly, at **Viana do Bolo** you can take a stroll through its traditional historic centre and contemplate a beautiful view of the O Vao dam.

View of Viana do Bolo, near the O Vao dam.

Fiestas in Viana do Bolo.

Panoramic view of the Sanctuary of As Ermidas.

O Bolo. Santuario de As Ermidas.